The Complete*ly*

Useless

Dictionary of

Higher Education

Also By Ilana S. Lehmann, Ph.D.

All You Need to Know About Disability

is on Star Trek

Dear Student: Inside the Twisted Mind

of an Exasperated Professor

The Completely Useless Dictionary of Higher Education

Ilana S. Lehmann, Ph.D.

Mind Meld Media

The Completely Useless Dictionary of Higher Education. Copyright 2015 by Mind Meld Media, LLC. All rights reserved. Printed in the United States of America. No part of this book may be used or reproduced in any manner whatsoever without the written permission of the publisher. Mind Meld Media, is a Limited Liability Corporation in the state of Delaware with its principal offices at 5313 NE 66th Ave G55, Vancouver, WA 98661.

Edited by Susan Frager
Art design by Jay Arnold at www.thelogonom.com

Library of Congress Control Number: 2015900595

Lehmann, Ilana S., 1961 -
 Dear Student: The Completely Useless Dictionary
 of Higher Education / Ilana S. Lehmann
 p. cm
 ISBN 978-0-9904540-5-2

All rights reserved.
Printed in the United States of America.

For Susie Derkins and Hobbes

*With special appreciation
to Sophie and Spencer*

PREFACE

According to my grandmother, the definition of a minute is determined by what side of the bathroom door you are on. While teaching graduate students, it occurred to me that the definition of certain words depends upon which side of the lectern the person stands. For example, take the word "syllabus." As a professor, I spend hours writing a syllabus for each course and I detail every aspect of the course trying to anticipate many of the questions students will have. My students seem to see a syllabus as an old-fashioned handout distributed by professors on the first day of class with the same information as the syllabuses from other classes.

From my perspective as the professor, it appears the only time students read the syllabus is when they need to find a loophole in the late work policy. College administrators view the syllabus as a document required by accreditation bodies, a contract between the professor and the student to be used as the basis for deciding grade appeals. Administrators treat these documents as if they were written on stone tablets. As a result, the average course syllabus has grown into a wordy tome that would make a lawyer proud.

Inspired by "The Devil's Dictionary" written by Ambrose Bierce in 1911, "The Completely Useless Dictionary of Higher Education" is a satirical reference book, written to entertain both academician and pupil.

Administrators are well-known for six-figure salaries and a complete lack of a sense of humor, so I doubt they will like this book.

Rather than using standard abbreviations for the parts of speech, (i.e. noun (*n*), verb (*v*), etc.), I use the following abbreviations to denote the role of the person defining the word: Professor (*pf.*), Student (*st.*), and Administrator (*adm.*).

On a few occasions, I consider *my* definition of the word to be the only one necessary. After all, I was a student before I had an office in the Ivory Towers.

A: 1. (*pf.*) The grade that represents near perfect answers or completeness of an assignment. Usually corresponding to 90% or above.

2. (*st.*) The grade deserved by students who turn in any work.

3. (*adm.*) A is the new C.

ABD: [All But Dissertation] 1. (*pf.*) A means whereby graduate students erroneously think other people know they only have a dissertation to write before they can demand to be addressed as "Doctor."

2. (*st.*) A type of academic purgatory in which a doctoral student has passed all coursework and preliminary examinations, but has not finished the dissertation. [see TIME OUT].

3. (*adm.*) A source of tuition from students who don't take up physical space in a classroom.

Abridge: 1. (*pf.*) The means of making something shorter.

2. (*st.*) The means of crossing over something, such as bodies of water.

3. (*adm.*) A source of toll money.

Absent: 1. (*pf.*) The opposite of being in the classroom.

2. (*st.*) The inability to come to class due to some *unforeseen circumstance* such as a wedding, birthday party, or football game.

3. (*adm.*) Showing that someone is not paying attention to what is being said: *The Provost answered with an absent smile.*

Absolute: 1. (*pf.*) A qualifier of truth by students. For example: The *absolute truth* about their absence from class, which usually involves the student definition.

2. (*st.*) The brand name of a vodka.

Abstract: 1. (*pf.*) The part of an article that tells the reader whether or not the study is relevant to a specific assignment.

2. (*st.*) An art form for people who can't make their art realistic.

Absurdity: 1. (*pf.*) The notion that you can get an extension on a research paper due to a football game or bachelor party.

2. (*st.*) The notion that you would spend time on schoolwork during Spring Break.

3. (*adm.*) The notion that a professor would be allowed to spend all of their grant money on their research.

Academia: The only place where productivity is measured in hours, and procrastination in years.

Academic: 1. (*pf.*) A highly educated person who engages in research and service while enlightening the minds of students.

2. (*st.*) A person who can over-complicate a bag of dirt.

A genius is someone who takes a complex thing and makes it look simple. An academic does the opposite. – Robert Fanney

3. (*adm.*) A person who thinks they are an expert at everything because they are highly educated about one thing.

Academic Dishonesty: 1. (*pf.*) A fancy expression for plagiarizing or cheating.

2. (*st.*) Copying someone else's test answers.

3. (*adm.*) When professors lie on their expense reports.

Academy: A school of special instruction such as a police academy. Not to be confused with Khan Academy where genetically engineered madmen learn about becoming tyrannical super humans.

Acceptance: 1. (*pf.*) The hard-fought battle of being allowed the privilege of publishing an article without any receiving any monetary compensation for the work.

2. (*st.*) The letter you receive telling you that you can apply for financial aid at this college.

3. (*adm.*) The realization on the part of professors that research grants belong to the university.

Accountability: 1. (*pf.*) A form of trustworthiness generally based on the records one keeps. A form of buttocks coverage.

2. (*st.*) The ability to count.

3. (*adm.*) The condition of being able to justify taking about half of research grant money under the guise of "overhead," (such as pencils, paper, copiers, etc.)

Accounting: A fancy name for a degree in bookkeeping.

Accreditation: 1. (*pf.*) A clever scam in which colleges and universities pay other people to scrutinize their syllabuses and faculty qualifications in order to advertise their programs as *accredited*. Meaningless in the real world, unless you need a professional license. (see LICENSURE)

Achievement: 1. (*pf.*) A goal that has been reached by hard work and ability rather than finding a loophole in the syllabus. Occasionally involved in GPAs, honors, and awards.

2. (*st.*) A level of play in video games that are unlocked by meeting unspecified criteria.

3. (*adm.*) Finding that loophole in the union contract which allows pay increases to be postponed.

Acknowledgement: 1. (*pf.*) In dissertations, this section usually goes on and on for pages and pages where everyone including the student's cat is thanked for their support.

2. (*st.*) A hat tip towards someone who helped you reach your goal. In a Master's thesis, this is usually where the author thanks the parents or spouse.

3. (*adm.*) Congratulating a professor for exceeding the requirements of the job–which is a requirement for tenure and promotion. The acknowledgment usually is a letter printed on high-quality paper with no monetary component.

2. (*st.*) Getting credit for having done something.

(*adm.*) A selling point for universities, which proves the worth of their programs by the approval of an outside group.

Adjunct Professor: 1. (*pf.*) An instructor with a graduate degree (M.S. or Ph.D.) who accepts slave wages, without benefits or permanent status, in exchange for not being required to produce uncompensated work products such as publications, committee service, and grant proposals. (see TENURE)

2. (*st.*) Not a real professor.

3. (*adm.*) Professors who share offices with other professors or graduate assistants.

Administration: 1. (*pf.*) The non-teaching, non-research staff at a university who decides who gets credit for activities, and who receives blame for mistakes. The largest part of the university payroll.

2. (*st.*) The people who work in the buildings without classrooms.

3. (*adm.*) The people who make the big decisions.

Admissions: 1. (*pf.*) A committee where professors select students to attend their program (see ADMISSIONS COMMITTEE).

2. (*st.*) The process of asking a college to take the parents' hard-earned money to pay the student's tuition.

3. (*adm.*) Necessary if the student wants to apply for student loans in order that the student may travel on spring breaks.

Admissions Committee: 1. (*pf.*) A group of lower-ranked professors who decide if an applicant can be useful to their own agendas (research or political). Historically similar to the deliberations of slave owners making decisions about the usefulness of slaves being offered for sale.

2. (*st.*) The faculty who invite applicants to campus for interviews and tours.

Advanced Placement: 1. (*pf.*) Moving a topic up on the committee meeting agenda.

2. (*st.*) Sitting in the front row of a classroom.

3. (*adm.*) A special high school course where students receive college credit for successfully passing.

Advisor: 1. (*pf.*) The person who helps a student with academic planning, including such inside information as what degree requires the least number of math courses.

2. (*st.*) The people in the academic advising center who know what is going on, not to be confused with the faculty member who consistently says, *I will look into that for you*, because they don't know anything about advising.

Agriculture: A degree program for farmers and gardeners.

Alcohol: 1. (*pf.*) Fuel for grading papers late at night.

2. (*st.*) A bonding chemical for undergraduate students.

3. (*adm.*) An elixir to inspire awkward people to dance.

All-nighter: 1. *(pf.)* The practice of reading a decade's worth of research and staying up all night writing a research proposal in order to meet a deadline that has been known for over three months.

2. *(st.)* The practice of reading a semester's worth of material and staying up all night studying for an examination, the date of which has been known for weeks. (see CRAMMING)

Alumni: 1. *(pf.)* Previous students who continue to ask for letters of recommendation even though you haven't seen them in decades.

2. *(st.)* A group responsible for sending boring magazines and requests for money.

3. *(adm.)* Previous students at the college who are now forever considered a source of donations and dues.

Anatomy: The study of naked bodies.

Anthropology: 1. *(pf.)* A doctoral degree which allows you to teach others anthropology.

2. (*st.*) At the bachelor's level, an anthropology degree should be kept secret if you want a paying job.

Apologize: 1. (*pf.*) An expression of regret for doing something wrong. Not to be confused with rationalizing why you did it.

2. (*st.*) An expression designed to convince the professor that you are remorseful when all you really want is to manipulate the situation.

Appeal: 1. (*pf.*) Challenging a professor to prove that a grade is appropriate in the hopes that the professor did not maintain a complete record of the student's lack of effort.

2. (*st.*) Referring to the outside of an apple or banana.

3. (*adm.*) A formal request by a student to tell their course professors they're full of shit.

Application: 1. (*pf.*) The form that is completed in order to be considered for admissions or financial aid.

2. (*st.*) A small computer program for smartphones.

3. (*adm.*) The process professors undertake in order to bring in research funding.

Archaeology: Legalized grave robbing.

"Archaeologists will date anything old." ~Author Unknown

Art: The opposite of science. Something that is practiced rather than perfected.

The art of medicine.

Ass: 1. (*pf.*) A student who arrives twenty minutes into the lecture and asks, "What did I miss?'

2. (*st.*) A professor who won't answer a direct question when you don't have time to read the syllabus.

3. (*adm.*) A professor who arrives late and leaves early during meetings.

Assignment: 1. (*pf.*) The basis for assigning a grade to a student after evaluating submitted work. Generally founded on the learning goals of the course.

2. (*st.*) The means professors use to keep the student busy that does not contribute to developing any skills needed in real life.

3. (*adm.*) The allocation of office space.

Assistant Professor: 1. (*pf.*) An untenured professor who works more than 74.5 hours per week and on the weekends.

2. (*st.*) An instructor who practices grade inflation owing to student course evaluation fears.

3. (*adm.*) A never-ending source of labor for serving on committees, writing grants, attending open house, publishing research, serving on boards, and teaching–a.k.a. department toady.

Associate Professor: 1. (*pf.*) The longest-held rank of an instructor; sandwiched between untenured vulnerability and Teflon-coated full professorship.

2. (*st.*) A professor who will no longer accept course work two weeks past the due date.

3. (*adm.*) More expensive than assistant professors, but easier to get rid of than full professors.

Associate's Degree: A credential indicating basic high school level proficiency in *most* courses.

Attrition: 1. (*pf.*) The rate at which students stop attending classes.

2. (*st.*) The opposite of nutrition.

3. (*adm.*) The rate at which rats die during research experiments.

Audit: 1. (*pf.*) A student's mystifying attendance in a course that does not count toward a degree.

2. (*st.*) A tactic used by blue-hairs so they have a place to go and hang out with young people.

3. (*adm.*) A source of senior citizen tuition.

B

B: 1. (*pf.*) A grade that means superior, but not outstanding work.

2. (*st.*) The grade that should be rounded to an A.

3. (*adm.*) A wake-up call to students that college is not the same as high school.

Baby: 1. (*pf.*) To handle with special care. *Untenured professors often baby students in order to receive positive comments on student evaluations.*

2. (*st.*) A cute, miniature human, who requires so much attention and care, that any *feeling* person would make allowances for the baby's parents during the pursuit of a college degree.

3. (*adm.*) A future source of legacy admissions.

Bachelor of Arts: An undergraduate college degree with a liberal arts emphasis that makes the student minimally qualified for working in a high profile position at a coffee bistro.

Bachelor of Science: An undergraduate college degree with a science emphasis and only pursued by students who can pass more than one math course. At times, a B. S. degree is self-explanatory.

Backpedal: 1. (*pf.*) A survival skill for the untenured.

2. (*st.*) A means of braking on a one-speed bicycle.

3. (*adm.*) To retreat from or reverse one's previous stand on a matter.

Basketball: A game where the players make shots and dunk their balls.

Bath: A tub of water where students drown their expensive cell phones in order to avoid emailing the professor when the Internet is down.

Battle: 1. (*pf.*) A sustained fight between large organized forces. When between the administration and the faculty, the condition of being organized is debatable.

2. (*st.*) The action in a first-person shooter game.

3. (*adm.*) A fight or tenacious struggle to achieve or resist something.

The battles over office space and merit pay were gruesome.

Beard: 1. (*pf.*) A hairy facial accessory for a male professor that identifies him as an unconventional scholar.

2. (*st.*) A hairy facial accessory for baby-faced male students worried about looking too young to get a date.

3. (*adm.*) A means of hiding the sexual orientation by someone who thinks no one knows he is gay.

Beer: 1. (*pf.*) A food group among undergraduate students.

2. (*st.*) An essential fluid to the undergraduate experience, which serves as a source of beautification when the bar is closing.

3. (*adm.*) A source of revenue at football games.

Beg: A fallback strategy employed by students when they learn they did not earn an A in a course. (see CURVE)

Bibliography: The list of sources students claim they read for the course even though it would take an average reader more than four years to finish.

Bigot: The only type of person you do not have to tolerate in academia.

Biology: The only science where multiplication is the same thing as division.

Blackboard: 1. (*pf.*) An Internet platform used for teaching. A fountain of frustration, irritation, and exasperation.

2. (*st.*) Another name for an antique chalkboard.

Bookstore: 1. (*pf.*) The place next to the coffee shop.

2. (*st.*) The retail outlet where the required textbook that costs $150 at the beginning of the semester, can be sold back at the end of the semester for enough money to buy a cappuccino at the coffee shop next door.

3. (*adm.*) A source of revenue where students' parents purchase items with the university logo to advertise where their money is being spent.

Botany: 1. (*pf.*) The scientific study of foliage where you learn which plants have the highest THC content.

2. (*st.*) What you ask when your roommate returns from shopping.

"Botany is the science in which plants are known by their aliases." (Anonymous; quoted in M. Goran, *A Treasury of Science Jokes*, 1986, p. 49.)

Boundary: 1. (*pf.*) The point at which something ends. In academia, boundaries are generally personal boundaries such as refusing to answer a call from a student at two in the morning. Exercised more by those with tenure than those without.

2. (*st.*) The expectation that professors will not read a student's Facebook page.

3. (*adm.*) A line that marks the limits of an area, such as the boundary between on-campus and off-campus.

Brain: 1. (*pf.*) The part of the body used by students to obtain a college degree.

2. (*st.*) The part of the body college students must protect from overuse.

3. (*adm.*) The smartest student in the class.

Budget: 1. (*pf.*) An estimation of how much money will remain from a grant after the administration removes their cut. An exaggerated amount of money that was requested to cover the actual cost of conducting the research.

2. (*st.*) An allowance of money set aside for a specific purpose.

I need to include airline tickets in my Spring Break budget.

3. (*adm.*) An adjective that describes something that is inexpensive or cheaper. For example, budget hotel, budget car, adjunct professor.

Bursar: The office which is considered as Santa Claus at the beginning of the semester when financial aid checks are distributed, and acts as an IRS collections office at the end of the semester when library fines and parking tickets must be paid in order to register for the next semester.

Business: A college major that teaches subjects related to commerce and banking–for students who are better at math than ethics.

C: 1. (*pf.*) The grade that means the work is of average or satisfactory quality. Corresponds to a correct percentage of between seventy to seventy-nine percent.

2. (*st.*) An insult.

3. (*adm.*) The grade necessary to keep football players academically eligible.

Cafeteria: 1. (*pf.*) A dispensary for coffee and a last resort for food.

2. (*st.*) The best place to eat on campus if you consider McDonald's a restaurant.

3. (*adm.*) A facility staffed by students on work-study, which feeds students who are working or studying.

Calendar: 1. (*pf.*) A means of scheduling topics and creating due dates for assignments. (see DUE DATES)

2. (*st.*) A means of keeping track of holidays, breaks, and other times in which classes do not meet, as well as shopping trips for when financial aid checks are disbursed.

3. (*adm.*) A tool the secretaries use to schedule appointments and meetings.

Campus: 1. (*pf.*) The grounds and buildings of a university, college, or school where young adults gather to experience excessive caffeine consumption, flirting, loud music, and to attend classes.

2. (*st.*) A place where students engage in similar activities to those in urban bars and pubs, but with the key difference being that parents provide financial support to be on campus.

3. (*adm.*) An incomplete set of buildings. The campus always needs more buildings and the existing buildings always need remodeling.

Canceled Class: 1. (*pf.*) The result of a professor suffering a heart attack or contracting a potentially fatal illness.

2. (*st.*) An unscheduled holiday.

3. (*adm.*) A missed day of vital instruction, which should be made up on the weekend.

Candidacy: The period of time that begins when the doctoral student's plan of study is approved, and ends when the student either graduates or dies from exhaustion–whichever comes first.

Cap And Gown: 1. (*pf.*) The only garment that can be both a tax deduction and a Harry Potter costume.

2. (*st.*) The required apparel worn at commencement exercises.

3. (*adm.*) Regalia worn at commencement and other formal ceremonies that cleverly disguises administrators as professors.

Capitalization: A means for Students to make Certain Words appear Important in their Papers even though Style Manuals have specific Rules for Capitalization.

Cat: A fuzzy creature capable of deleting computer files by unknown means, puking on keyboards just before due dates, and becoming seriously ill before midterms and finals.

Catalogue: 1. (*pf.*) A list of systematically arranged university courses including the list of pre-requisites.

2. (*st.*) A magazine-style shopping guide for spending financial aid checks.

Cell Phone: 1. (*pf.*) A portable telecommunications device used for phone conversations that disrupts classes and meetings by those who fail to silence the ringer.

2. (*st.*) A portable telecommunications device used to take pictures and send text messages during class. Rarely used for conversations by anyone under the age of thirty.

3. (*adm.*) The primary means students use to communicate.

Challenge: 1. (*pf.*) The struggle between grading a student's assignment accurately, while not damaging your rating on end of course evaluations. 2. (*st.*) The balance between getting the best grade possible while doing the least amount of work needed to achieve a good grade.

Chancellor: (*pf.*) The head of the government in some European countries. *In 1933, Adolf Hitler was appointed the Chancellor of Germany.*

2. (*st.*) The fancy name for the head of a university.

3. (*adm.*) The most visible and highest paid administrator, not to be confused with the amount of work production.

Cheerleader: 1. (*pf.*) Stereotypically viewed as weak students who, regardless of the weather, wear skimpy clothing to football games and encourage football players who are tossing around a two-pound ball.

2. (*st.*) Athletes who are capable of throwing and catching each other, while wearing costumes that make Playboy bunnies look overdressed.

3. (*adm.*) Future Hooters wait staff.

Chemistry: 1. (*pf.*) The only discipline in which alcohol is a solution.

2. (*st.*) A course similar to cooking except you should never lick the spoon.

Christmas: 1. (*pf.*) A winter holiday that isn't really a holiday because classes are already over. For single academics, it is a good day to work on manuscripts or update the syllabuses for the next semester. For academics with families, it is a time when the academic gets to talk to the people they live with, while not sitting behind a computer screen.

2. (*st.*) The reason to visit family, receive gifts, and get caught up on laundry.

3. (*adm.*) A winter holiday that doesn't entail any holiday pay for faculty. The best day to find parking on campus.

Citation: 1. (*pf.*) The means of documenting sources while writing research papers.

2. (*st.*) The document left on the windshield by campus police when your car is illegally parked. And something professors say they want on research papers.

3. (*adm.*) An award for excellence in teaching or research.

Clairvoyance: 1. (*pf.*) The paranormal power of seeing through excuses for absences and late assignments achieved by professors after they have taught for a minimum of two weeks.

2. (*st.*) The ability to know what is in a syllabus without reading it because they're all the same.

Class: 1. (*pf.*) A group of students meeting regularly to study a subject under the guidance of an instructor. Not to be confused with a study group which does not involve an instructor but may involve beer.

2. (*st.*) A group of students who meet regularly to catch up on much needed sleep.

3. (*adm.*) A grouping of donors based on the year they graduated. (e.g. Class of 2014.)

Classroom: 1. (*pf.*) The physical room or Internet equivalent where a professor attempts to impart information while entertaining their students in order to keep the students awake.

2. (*st.*) A place where you can relax after a strenuous night on the town.

Click: 1. (*pf.*) To emit or produce a slight sharp sound usually by pressing the left or right button on a mouse.

2. (*st.*) The sudden realization that an assignment is due, as in: *It just clicked; I have a paper due in two hours.*

Code of Conduct: 1. (*pf.*) The rules outlining proper behavior for college students with regards to their classroom conduct and communication with professors.

2. (*st.*) Talking quietly in the library.

3. (*adm.*) The policy that allows students and faculty to be dismissed if they embarrass the university.

Coffee: 1. (*pf.*) An organic suspension that provides fuel for late night grading, and helped Captain Janeway defeat the Borg.

2. (*st.*) Study juice.

3. (*adm.*) The liquid that circulates in the veins of administrators.

Comfort: (*pf.*) To soothe, console, and cheer.

2. (*st.*) In the Southern form, it provides 80 proof relaxation.

Commencement: 1. (*pf.*) A day-long process of wearing archaic costumes, listening to semi-famous people deliver boring speeches, and sitting on uncomfortable folding chairs because you are required to attend.

2. (*st.*) A day-long process of wearing archaic costumes, listening to semi-famous people deliver boring speeches, and sitting on uncomfortable folding chairs waiting for the thrilling seven-and-a-half seconds when you walk across the stage to shake hands with the chancellor and receive an empty diploma holder.

3. (*adm.*) The ceremonial transformation from students who pay tuition, into alumni who donate money to their university.

Committee: A group of people who keep minutes and waste hours.

Commuter College: A nonresidential college that differs from *community colleges* by virtue of providing degrees of B.S. (both definitions.)

Comprehensive Exam: 1. (*pf.*) An extensive examination taken by master's level students; given to measure proficiency in a major field of study.

2. (*st.*) Passage of this exam allows students to move into candidacy and go further into debt by borrowing more money to complete degree.

Computer: 1. (*pf.*) A sophisticated technology device which will reliably fail whenever due dates are imminent.

2. (*st.*) A backup for a smartphone.

Computer Science: The degree program where students learn how to turn caffeine into computer applications.

Continuing Education: A scam by professional organizations to require college graduates to continue to take classes.

Copy: 1. (*pf.*) To make a thing similar or identical to another. Often employed by students as a strategy for cheating.

2. (*st.*) A time management strategy whereby the student saves time by not creating something that has already been created by someone else.

May I copy your lecture notes?

3. (*adm.*) What copiers do.

Copyright: 1. (*pf.*) The exclusive legal right, given to the creator of the material, which establishes ownership of said material.

2. (*st.*) A pre-Internet concept that ignores the right of the people to copy anything they want including term papers, music, and videos.

If I found it, it is mine.

3. (*adm.*) The right of the university to collect revenues from certain work products created by naïve professors.

Counseling: A degree program for students who want to get paid for listening to others while occasionally nodding their heads.

Course buyout: The upside of conducting research whereby the faculty is paid not to teach a course.

Course evaluations: 1. (*pf.*) The source of grade inflation, nightmares, and denial of tenure.

2. (*st.*) A vehicle for revenge when a student isn't given an A.

3. (*adm.*) Customer satisfaction surveys.

Course number: 1. (*pf.*) A number assigned to college courses that indicates the department in which the course is taught, and the class of students for who the course is designed. (i.e. ENG 101 is a freshman English course.)

2. (*st.*) The order in which courses are arranged in the course catalog.

Course overload: 1. (*pf.*) Taking more courses in a given semester than is generally allowed by the school, resulting in a student who constantly asks for extensions and special consideration.

2. (*st.*) Taking more than the recommended number of courses in order to get through college as fast as possible. A strategy favored by students who already have the knowledge and simply lack the credentials.

3. (*adm.*) Courses taught by regular faculty during the summer which requires additional pay to the instructor.

Cramming: 1. (*pf.*) Fitting what takes days into hours. (see ALL-NIGHTER)

2. (*st.*) Fitting what was in a house into a dorm room.

Creative Writing: 1. (*pf.*) A research proposal.

2. (*st.*) An easy A.

3. (*adm.*) A union contract.

Credential: 1. (*pf.*) A document that states a person's qualifications.

2. (*st.*) A document proving a person's worth.

3. (*adm.*) For sale by universities under the label "diploma."

Credit hour: 1. (*pf.*) The unit of academic credit that represents the number of hours the class meets weekly, as well as approximately one fourth of the amount of time a student should spend on the course materials outside of class.

2. (*st.*) The number of hours a class meets each week.

3. (*adm.*) A tuition and fee billing unit.

Critique: 1. (*pf.*) A detailed analysis, usually involving a literary, philosophical, or theoretical publication.

2. (*st.*) Criticism on the part of the instructor, usually communicated by A, B, C, D, or F.

Current: 1. (*pf.*) Pertaining to relevant and recent research. Less than seven years old.

2. (*st.*) Pertaining to fashion and music. Less than seven days old.

3. (*adm.*) Pertaining to organizational structure. Less than seven hundred years old.

Curriculum: The means and methods by which student learning will be achieved as outlined in the syllabus. (see SYLLABUS)

Curve: 1. (*pf.*) Magical thinking on the part of students that a mathematical formula exists which turns a 37% into an A grade.

2. (*st.*) The only fair means of grading, which allows everyone to pass the course regardless of whether they learned anything.

D: 1. (*pf.*) A passing grade in undergraduate programs and non-passing grade in graduate schools.

2. (*st.*) The grade given in courses that interfere with sleep, parties, or vacations.

3. (*adm.*) The grade given to students that don't learn anything, but the professor doesn't want them to be in their class again.

Dance: A major for aspiring performers or choreographers who, after failing to find employment in the entertainment industry, wait tables until they complete a real college degree.

Data: 1. (*pf.*) Observations in a research study.

2. (*st.*) The android on Star Trek.

3. (*adm.*) The opinions of the powers-that-be.

Deadline: 1. (*pf.*) The absolute last day to turn in an assignment for credit.

2. (*st.*) An off-hand suggestion of when a professor wants an assignment turned in, subject to emergencies and well-made excuses.

3. (*adm.*) An absolute when applied to faculty, and a general guideline when applied to members of the administration.

Dean: 1. (*pf.*) The person who *requires* attendance at numerous long meetings, and then complains that there is not enough research being conducted by the faculty.

2. (*st.*) The person who will listen to the complaints of students (and their parents) and is capable of forcing a professor to pass a student even if the student has never attended a single class.

3. (*adm.*) The head of a college or department. As chief academic officer of the college, the Dean is

responsible for the academic, personnel, financial, and administrative affairs of the college.

Dean's list: 1. (*pf.*) A list of students made by a work study student in the Dean's office who have taken difficult courses such as Bowling 101 or Introduction to the Modern History of Motion Pictures.

2. (*st.*) A list of college students who usually have a B+ average or higher and is considered to be an achievement by parents and employers.

3. (*adm.*) List of tasks given to the work-study student in the Dean's office.

Death: 1. (*pf.*) The only valid reason for not attending a final exam.

2. (*st.*) The potential result of attending boring lectures.

3. (*adm.*) The only valid reason for not paying late fees.

Degree audit: 1. (*pf.*) A computer-generated analysis that assesses the student's academic progress towards a declared college degree.

2. (*st.*) A means of figuring out if changing majors would result in an earlier graduation. Often sought during the fifth year of a four-year degree program.

Denial: 1. (*pf.*) The belief that students will refrain from asking questions before checking the syllabus for the answers.

2. (*st.*) A river in Africa.

3. (*adm.*) The negative end to a tenure request.

Diploma: 1. (*pf.*) Required office wallpaper.

2. (*st.*) Certificate documenting the mastery of Google and Wikipedia.

3. (*adm.*) A receipt for tuition money.

Disappointment: 1. (*pf.*) Getting your office taken away because of a new hire.

2. (*st.*) Getting your graduate assistantship taken away because of a low GPA.

3. (*adm.*) Getting your secretary taken away because of a new hire.

Disbursement: 1. (*pf.*) Receiving the remaining few dollars from the large research grant, after the administration has taken most of the money for overhead costs.

2. (*st.*) Receiving the remaining money from the financial aid office after the administration has taken out the cost of tuition and fees.

3. (*adm.*) Pay day.

Discipline: 1. (*pf.*) A branch of knowledge, typically one studied at institutions of higher learning.

2. (*st.*) An alternative to Ritalin.

3. (*adm.*) The ability of professors to refrain from saying anything during interviews which will embarrass the university.

Discussion: 1. (*pf.*) The conversation that occurs when the professor is right, and continues until the students realize it.

2. (*st.*) The conversation that occurs when the student is right, and continues until the professor realizes it.

3. (*adm.*) A time-consuming activity engaged in by committee members prior to approving the proposal from the administration.

Dismissal: 1. (*pf.*) The end of your professional career.

2 (*st.*) The end of the school day.

3. (*adm.*) The end of a lawsuit.

Dissertation: 1. (*pf.*) The capstone of a doctoral education, which will only be read by the student's dissertation committee and possibly their family.

2. (*st.*) The most brilliant research on the planet, which will change life as we know it forever.

3. (*adm.*) The reason libraries have basements.

Distance learning: 1. (*pf.*) Online education courses taken by students with Internet access.

2. (*st.*) Sitting in the back of a classroom.

3. (*adm.*) Parking in one of the auxiliary parking lots.

Divorce: A common side-effect of attending graduate school. Usually filed just before an important assignment is due.

Dog: 1. (*pf.*) A furry creature with a mythical reputation for preferring homework assignments to food that smells like a meat product.

2. (*st.*) A domesticated mammal that typically has a long snout, an acute sense of smell, and a barking, howling, or whining voice which carries especially well when speaking on the phone.

3. (*adm.*) A creature capable of learning, but incapable of paying tuition.

Dorm room: 1. (*pf.*) A small room with beds where college students practice breaking rules regarding alcohol, drugs, and sex.

2. (*st.*) A small room with beds where strangers sleep together.

3. (*adm.*) A small room with beds where college students sleep.

Download: 1. (*pf.*) The transfer of computer files.

2. (*st.*) The way computers learn stuff.

3. (*adm.*) A means of saving on printing costs.

Drop: 1. (*pf.*) Another name for throat lozenges.

The Completely Useless Dictionary of Higher Education

2. (*st.*) A means of getting out of a class without losing all of your tuition money.

3. (*adm.*) What department chairs tend to do with the ball.

Due Date: 1. (*pf.*) A date during the semester when a student states her baby will be born and is the only day you can be certain the baby will not be delivered. Never occurs during vacations or semester breaks.

2. (*st.*) See DEADLINE.

3. (*adm,*) The date when budgets must be approved by the Board of Regents.

Earth Sciences: An all-embracing term for the sciences related to the planet Earth, as if anyone cares about other planets.

Easter: A religious holiday for celebrating colored eggs and chocolate bunnies. Often coincides with spring break.

Ecology: A degree program for tree huggers, whale watchers, environmentalists, recyclers, and hippies where they earn the right to be called scientists, too.

Economics: The discipline that teaches students how to predict nine of the next five recessions.

Ed.D.: A doctorate of education degree. Esteemed by many, scorned by many more.

Education: What professors think they provide, students think they want, and administrators think they sell.

Elective: 1. (*pf.*) Allegedly fun courses designed by professors to sell their most recent book.

2. (*st.*) A course chosen by the student as opposed to being required for a degree program. A good place to socialize, be entertained, and relax. Sometimes referred to as a "GPA booster."

3. (*adm.*) A means of collecting tuition for courses that don't advance a student's degree program.

Email: 1. (*pf.*) Delayed communication when a professor asks a student a question.

2. (*st.*) Instant communication for student questions.

3. (*adm.*) A means of sending office memos to everyone, which provides a record that *they have been told*.

Engineering: A degree program for people who get overly excited over boring things.

English: 1. (*pf.*) Where native English speakers study their own language in the hopes they will learn how to use it properly.

2. (*st.*) A college major for grammar Nazis.

3. (*adm.*) The most likely department to be cut.

Entrance exam: 1. (*pf.*) A means of determining whether a student is ready to take a rigorous course usually in a highly technical field such as mathematics, engineering, or physics. (a.k.a. proof the student is not stupid.)

2. (*st.*) A source of black market revenue.

3. (*adm.*) Finding a place to park.

Essay: 1. (*pf.*) A writing assignment on a specific subject graded for content, spelling, grammar, and organization.

2. (*st.*) Writing a specific number of pages or words which are randomly divided into paragraphs.

3. (*adm.*) A test of writing skills for incoming freshmen.

Eternity: The time spent in a statistics course.

Ethics: 1. (*pf.*) The reason students shouldn't cheat on their course work.

2. (*st.*) The reason professors should make all exams open book. After all, students paid for the course and the book.

3. (*adm.*) An office on the bottom floor.

Excuse: 1. (*pf.*) What students say about assignments that are late.

2. (*st.*) What professors say about grades being posted late.

Expert: 1. (*pf.*) A person with skills or knowledge in a specific area. Sometimes used to describe a professor.

2. (*st.*) A former pert.

Extra credit: 1. (*pf.*) An opportunity to demonstrate mastery of course materials previously considered deficit. Provided at the discretion of a professor.

2. (*st.*) The right of students to improve their grade when the course work has been too hard and the professor has been too picky. (see GRADE)

3. (*adm.*) A guaranteed increase in a student's grade rarely granted by tenured professors.

Extracurricular: 1. (*pf.*) Student activities that provide a well-rounded education for students (e.g. debate, chorus, plays, and sports).

2. (*st.*) Everything not done in a classroom (e.g. shopping, drinking, flirting, and sex).

3. (*adm.*) Outside the normal routine, especially those provided by a job or marriage.

F

F: 1. (*pf.*) The grade given to students who fail to demonstrate mastery of the course content.

2. (*st.*) Evidence of the biased attitude of a professor.

3. (*adm.*) The grade given students who stopped attending but forgot to drop the course.

Facebook: A website where students disclose personal information that an employer or a school administrator could never legally ask for.

Faculty: 1. (*pf.*) The teaching staff at a college or university divided into two groups: Adjunct and tenured or tenure-track faculty.

2. (*st.*) A mental or physical ability.

3. (*adm.*) The teaching staff at a college which are usually divided into three groups: (1) [tenured] underworked and overpaid (2) [tenure-tracked] overworked, underpaid, but with promises of tenure, and [adjunct] overworked and underpaid, without delusions that life will ever get any better than this.

FAFSA (*Free Application for Federal Student Aid*) 1. (*pf.*) Another program paid for by taxpayers.

2. (*st.*) Free money for college.

3. (*adm.*) Free money for colleges.

Family and Consumer Sciences: A degree program for students who need to be taught how to cook, sew, and clean house because their moms were too busy doing other things to teach them. The modern name for Home Economics (formerly known as an MRS degree.)

FAQ: (Frequently Asked Questions) A webpage that serves as the syllabus of the website. Unlike a syllabus, however, people actually read the FAQ.

Fees: A method colleges use to hide the cost of attendance. The fees can be as much as six times the cost of tuition. Fees are charged for such educational necessities as: "Seismic/Safety," "Academic Excellence," and "Student voice and Empowerment."

"Beware of little expenses; a small leak will sink a great ship." -Benjamin Franklin

FERPA: (Family Educational Rights and Privacy Act): 1. (*pf.*) The only thing stopping your instructor from telling your parents on you.

2. (*st.*) Facebook Entertainment Rights and Partying Anecdotes?

3. (*adm.*) A reason to hire six more administrators.

Finals: 1. (*pf.*) Acronym: Finding Idiots Never Actually Learned Shit

2. (*st.*) Acronym: Fuck, I Never Actually Learned Shit

Financial Aid: 1. (*pf.*) University funds, start-up funds, and internal research grants. (Not to be confused with salary or consulting fees.)

2. (*st.*) Pell grants, work-study, graduate assistantships, student loans, scholarships, and money from parents. (Not to be confused with work or earnings.)

3. (*adm.*) Any source of money used to pay tuition and fees as well as tax money and block grants.

Fine arts: A college degree in being artsy-fartsy as opposed to a liberal arts program.

First person: 1. (*pf.*) Referring to oneself in writing by using the pronouns "I" or "me."

2. (*st.*) Beginning of the line at Starbucks.

3. (adm.) A pioneer.

She was the first person in her family to graduate from college.

Football: In America, it is the game where either 20 college students or 20 millionaires try to get their hands on one strangely shaped ball. In the rest of the world, it is the game Americans call soccer.

Foreign Languages: A college major where you learn to swear in several tongues.

Freshman: 1. (*pf.*) A first-year college student.

2. (*st.*) The guys who ask others what they are wearing in online courses.

Fulbright: 1. (*pf.*) One of the most prestigious awards programs worldwide, operating in over 150 countries where faculty receive funds to study and conduct research. It takes the place of a beauty pageant or talent show for faculty members.

2. (*st.*) The student version (Fulbright-Hays) is a fully-paid study abroad program that takes students to countries they would never pick for a vacation.

Funeral: 1. (*pf.*) A traditional excuse for missing classes especially when an assignment is due or an exam is being given.

2. (*st.*) The best place to hide from class when there is an assignment due.

3. (*adm.*) The only place where people will give you evil looks if you ask for the WiFi password.

Geek: 1. (*pf.*) Someone who is generally highly knowledgeable, even to the point of obsession, about topics such as Star Trek or Doctor Who.

2. (*st.*) The guy or girl you call when your computer needs fixing.

General Education: The education of generals.

Geography: The college major where being able to color within the lines is considered a job skill.

Geology: Where rocks are not categorized as "Classic," "Punk," or "Hard."

Gerontology: The degree program where you start out studying old people, and end up being studied by young people.

Google: 1. (*pf.*) An Internet search engine.

2. (*st.*) The primary method of conducting research online.

3. (*adm.*) A method of finding funny cat videos.

GPA (Grade Point Average): 1. (*pf.*) The basis for awarding honors at graduation.

2. (*st.*) A minimum requirement for continuing to receive financial aid while attending college.

3. (*adm.*) (Graduate Program Advisor) The person who convinces soon-to-be college graduates to stay in school and pay graduate school tuition in order to receive an advanced degree.

Grade: 1. (*pf.*) The level of mastery demonstrated by the student at the end of the course.

2. (*st.*) The evaluation of student work that takes into account the amount of time and effort involved in completing the assignment with consideration to the student's marital status, employment status, stress levels, parental status, pet destructiveness, and the health of parents,

grandparents, in-laws, aunts, uncles, nieces, and nephews.

3. (*adm.*) The most common basis for an appeal.

Graduate: An unemployed person who is not eligible for any type of financial assistance except from their parents.

Graduate Assistant: A graduate student who has the privilege of working nearly as hard as an assistant professor in exchange for a tuition waiver, a stipend, and excessive caffeine consumption.

Graduate school: 1. (*pf.*) A refuge for insecure college graduates, who want to hang out with insecure faculty, in order to feel less insecure about their insecure future.

2. (*st.*) A place to hide from work, parents, and responsibility.

3. (*adm.*) A pool of students that provide slave labor in the form of "graduate assistants."

Grammar: An obsolete practice for people who don't use Twitter or text on their cell phones.

Grant: An elusive, if not mythical, quest for money that can be a determining factor in a tenure decision.

Greek: 1. (*pf.*) Pertaining to Greece.

2. (*st.*) Fraternities and sororities; where you are a lifelong source of donations.

3. (*adm.*) All the concerns of the faculty.

Group Project: 1. (*pf.*) An assignment given to five people in which two of them do the work, and everyone gets the same grade.

2. (*st.*) A time to relax and watch those who really care do all the work.

3. (*adm.*) In the business world, it is known as "committee work."

Handout: 1. (*pf.*) Printed information provided to students.

2. (*st.*) The opposite of hand-in.

3. (*adm.*) Something given to a needy person or student.

History: A college major for people interested in studying dead people.

Hold: 1. (*pf.*) A strategy to delay talking to a person on the phone.

2. (*st.*) Your capacity to consume alcohol.

3. (*adm.*) Preventing a student's registration until they have paid their bill.

Holiday: An excuse not to attend a class.

Homecoming: Started in 1911 by Mizzou, in which alumni were invited to buy tickets to attend a football game. Stolen by high schools for the night when a King and Queen are crowned.

Honeymoon: A personal vacation commonly following a wedding in which a student feels entitled to avoid classes, assignments, exams, and other scholarly activities. Also known as a personal vacation for the purpose of engaging in a lot of sex. Never attended by tenure-track faculty.

Hood: 1. (*pf.*) An oddly shaped accessory to the academic robe worn by masters and doctoral graduates, which identifies the school where they earned their degree.

2. (*st.*) A slang expression for a "residential neighborhood."

3. (*adm.*) A covering for the head that is attached to a jacket or sweatshirt.

Humanities: 1. (*pf.*) The branches of learning that investigate human constructs and concerns, as opposed to anything practical.

2. (*st.*) A cool program which focuses on literature, art, and philosophy rather than on skills which could be used in the workplace.

3. (*adm.*) Classes which involve inquiry into consciousness, values, ideas, and ideals as they seek to describe how experiences shape our understanding of the world while increasing the amount of tuition paid by the student.

Hypothesis: 1. (*pf.*) A theory about what the scientist expects to find within a specific context, that which is tested in experimental research.

2. (*st.*) A stoned pothesis.

3. (*adm.*) A wild guess by a tenure-track professor.

I

Illness: 1. (*pf.*) An excuse for not attending class, submitting assignments, or taking exams.
2. (*st.*) The feeling that results when a student suddenly realizes they are unprepared for the day.
3. (*adm.*) The primary excuse for everything not done on time.

Immature: An adjective that describes the politics in academia.

Incomplete: A second chance at passing a course when a student has blown off assignments during the regular semester.

Inconvenience: A word used by students to refer to their behavior when they are being a royal pain in the ass.

Independent Study: Paying college tuition for a course of where the student is both the instructor and the student, but not the evaluator.

Institutional Review Board: A group of researchers who protect other researchers from doing research.

Instructor: 1. (*pf.*) The title given those who teach college courses without a Ph.D.

2. (*st.*) The title given professionals in the field who teach at colleges.

3. (*adm.*) The bottom of the faculty pay scale.

International Student: 1. (*pf.*) The student whose paper is free from spelling, grammar, and style errors because they look up what they don't know.

2. (*st.*) The classmate who sets the curve and talks funny.

3. (*adm.*) A customer who pays almost five times as much tuition as a local student and usually are better students.

Internship: A clever scheme by employers where students work without pay in exchange for the experience of answering the phone and making coffee.

IT Help Desk: Another function of the untenured professor. Open 24/7.

Jail 1. (*pf.*) A valid excuse to missing class. Valid, but not excused.

2. (*st.*) The primary motivation to have a designated driver.

3. (*adm.*) The most embarrassing place for a faculty member to spend the night.

Job: 1. (*pf.*) The reason most students go to college.

2. (*st.*) Where people who aren't in college go during the day.

3. (*adm.*) The reason budget meetings are held.

Journal: 1. (*pf.*) A company that publishes (without remuneration) the manuscripts of researchers after unpaid reviewers have deemed them worthy. The journal then sells issues back to the university, where the researcher is employed.

2. (*st.*) What people used to write in before there was Facebook, Tumblr, and Pinterest.

3. (*adm.*) A publishing hierarchy for determining tenure.

Journalism: 1. (*pf.*) A degree program for students who want to tell others what to think.

2. (*st.*) A major that leads to working as a news anchor, foreign correspondent, or investigative reporter.

3. (*adm.*) A major for students with delusions of grandeur. (see second definition)

Junior: 1. (*pf.*) Professors without tenure.

2. (*st.*) The class of students who are entering their third year in college.

3. (*adm.*) Professors without tenure.

K

Kappa: 1. (*pf.*) Greek letter used in the names of fraternities and sororities including Kappa Sigma, Kappa Delta, and Kappa Kappa Gamma.

2. (*st.*) The Super Mario character who looks like a turtle and his shells can be thrown at things.

3. (*adm.*) A container for coffee.

Karma: 1. (*pf.*) An action, according to Eastern philosophy, that will have repercussions in this life or the one after.

2. (*st.*) The belief that professors who don't give all students As should not be granted tenure.

3. (*adm.*) The reason to offer vegetarian dishes in the cafeteria.

Keg 1. (*pf.*) A small barrel.

2. (*st.*) A small barrel of beer traditionally celebrated at college parties.

3. (*adm.*) 58.6738827 liters.

Key: 1. (*pf.*) A vital part.

Reading the syllabus is a key part of attending college.

2. (*st.*) A small metal instrument for locking and unlocking doors, guaranteed not to work if being chased by zombies.

3. (*adm.*) A button on a keyboard.

Kinesiology: A science of body movement which includes mechanics and anatomy. It was created so there would be one health discipline that begins with the letter K.

Kirk: 1. (*pf.*) The Church of Scotland.

2. (*st.*) The captain on the Star Trek series my grandfather watched.

L

Lab: 1. (*pf.*) An academic period devoted to work or study.

2. (*st.*) A room where students are allowed to play with fire, dissect animals, grow cannabis, and *accidentally* blow stuff up.

3. (*adm.*) A large breed of dog.

Late: (*pf.*) The opposite of being on time.

2. (*st.*) Any time after 2 am weekdays.

Law (School): A degree program for students who want to learn how to measure life in billable hours.

Learning outcomes: The part of the syllabus where the professor lists what the accreditation committee told them to teach in the course. (see ACCREDITATION)

Lecture: "The art of transferring information from the notes of the professor to the notes of the student without passing through the minds of either." ~Author Unknown

Letter of Recommendation: 1. (*pf.*) A carefully drafted letter to advance a student for a job or attendance at graduate school without revealing that the student was always late and barely passed the course.

2. (*st.*) A right of students to have their professors make them sound good to potential employers or graduate school admission committees.

3. (*adm.*) One of the required pieces of paper to be contained in the faculty's personnel file, but never read by anyone.

Liberal Arts: The study of nothing specific and everything in general. A college degree favored by restaurant servers and security guards.

Library: 1. (*pf.*) A place to conduct literature reviews for journal publications.

2. (*st.*) The building on campus with the strongest WiFi and coffee.

3. (*adm.*) A home for theses and dissertations.

Licensure: A conspiracy in which testing companies have convinced the powers-that-be that passing their tests guarantees a basic level of competence. If you did not graduate from an accredited program, you are usually prohibited from even taking the test. (see ACCREDITATION)

Linguistics: A degree program for people who loved diagramming sentences in high school. It qualifies the student for a bartending career explaining syntax to drunks.

Literature Review: 1. (*pf.*) The text of a scholarly paper, which reviews the current knowledge on the topic and allows the author to cite his or her own work in an attempt to establish a reputation as an expert in the field.

2. (*st.*) The part of a scholarly paper that doesn't include a lot of statistics.

Lower Division: 1. (*pf.*) Classes designed to be taken by first and second year college students.

2. (*st.*) Where student-athletes play sports but will not be drafted by a professional team (i.e. NCAA Division I).

M

Major: 1. (*pf.*) A specialization in a subject or field at a university.

2. (*st.*) A code for identifying your future occupation.

"I am an education major" means "I want to be a teacher someday because I don't want to work during the summer."

Management: 1. (*pf.*) To be in charge. i.e. Classroom management: similar to herding cats.

2. (*st.*) Succeed in attaining one's goals. i.e. Time management: historically, when people sacrificed their sleep, food and personal life they were called saints, now they're called college students.

3. (*adm.*) To have control of something. i.e. Anger management: an unnecessary activity if people would do as they are told.

Marriage: When a man loses his bachelor's degree and a woman gets her master's degree.

Mascot: 1. (*pf.*) A scarf-like garment worn around the neck, which is more comfortable than a tie, to make professors look distinguished.

2, (*st.*) The cool guy at the football game who runs around and acts silly while hiding his identify in a huge costume.

3. (*adm.*) The overpaid work-study student who receives a stipend for running around the field acting like an idiot.

Master's Degree: Graduate school preparation for becoming better educated than the other people who can't find jobs.

Math: "Mental Abuse To Humans" ~Author Unknown

Mathematics: The only discipline where a child can have 24 cookies, eat 18 of them, and no one asks why.

Medicine (Medical School): A school which leads to a medical degree and a six-figure student loan. Usually attempted by people who want to say, "Trust me, I'm the doctor" but do not own a TARDIS.

Medieval Studies: An academic study of the Middle Ages. Not to be confused with Mid-evil Studies which are studies about things that are between twenty-five percent and seventy-five percent evil, or Middle Age Studies which are about people between forty-five and sixty years old.

Meeting: 1. (*pf.*) An assembly of people for the purpose of reaching consensus on the decision already made by someone in authority.

2. (*st.*) An appointment with a professor near the end of the term in which the student pleads for leniency, or an extra credit project.

3. (*adm.*) An assembly of chosen faculty members who approve decisions that have already been made by the administration.

Mentor: 1. (*pf.*) An experienced and trusted advisor.

2. (*st.*) The only professor who understands and helps students.

3. (*adm.*) A person whose position is higher in the food chain.

Microbiology: The study of germs by a very small biologist.

Midterm: 1. (*pf.*) The middle of the semester when half the grading is done, but the lamest excuses are yet to come.

2. (*st.*) The exam taken at the midpoint of the semester that produces a feeling that reading the textbook and going to class might have been important. The feeling frequently returns during finals week.

3. (*adm.*) The point in the semester when the number of research proposals decline.

Minor: 1. (*pf.*) Lesser in importance. *Moving classrooms is a minor inconvenience compared to rescheduling the time.*

2. (*st.*) The study of a secondary subject by undergraduate students, which makes them a near expert in a secondary field. *I think I will minor in Frisbee golf.*

3. (*adm.*) A student who is under the age of full legal responsibility and the reason to have resident assistants in dorms.

Mortarboard: 1. (*pf.*) An academic cap consisting of a headpiece with a broad flat projecting square worn by graduates at commencement. (see CAP AND GOWN)

2. (*st.*) The engine that makes the boat go.

Mother: 1. (*pf.*) The only person on Earth who cannot be used as a reference for college admissions.

2. (*st.*) The only person on Earth who believes you when you claim it wasn't your fault.

3. (*adm.*) The only person on Earth who will bail you out of jail.

Mouse: 1. (*pf.*) A small rodent used in psychology experiments when undergraduate students are unavailable.

2. (*st.*) The computer input device for playing games, creating graphics, sending emails, and liking your friend's posts on Facebook.

3. (*adm.*) The computer input device used while editing documents such as agendas.

Music: The class where students take notes about notes on notebook paper.

NCAA: The National Collegiate Athletic Association, a so-called nonprofit association that regulates student athletes and, until the 1984 Supreme Court decision, held the television broadcast rights to games and a significant share of the revenues.

Never mind: 1. (*pf.*) An expression usually said under the breath, which indicates the realization the other person is too stupid to understand.

2. (*st.*) An expression, usually said under the breath, which indicates the realization that the other person is too pig-headed to understand.

3. (*adm.*) An expression frequently said to administrators by busy people.

Night class: 1. (*pf.*) A class which takes place during the evening for people who work during the day.

2. (*st.*) A class which takes place during the evening for people who sleep during the day.

3. (*adm.*) Classes for faculty and students who hate parking during the day.

Non-credit courses: Courses offered through continuing education departments where the student attends classes and receives no grade, no credit towards a degree, and pays no tuition, only fees. Usually attended by people who don't have a life.

Non-traditional student: 1. (*pf.*) A student who did not go to college immediately after high school. Classification pertains to age, part-time status, and the wearing of suits to class.

2. (*st.*) Old farts pretending to be cool college students.

3. (*adm.*) Students with real-life experience.

Notes: 1. (*pf.*) The art of taking pen to paper and doodling during faculty meetings in order to give the appearance of writing down important information from the meeting.

2. (*st.*) The ancient practice of writing to look attentive during class. The practice has been replaced with laptops and smartphones used for note taking while shopping, posting to Facebook, and watching funny cat videos.

3. (*adm.*) The handout given before a meeting because faculty cannot be trusted to write down what they need to remember.

Nursing: A degree program for people who want to take care of others while neglecting their own health, family, and income.

Oceanography: The degree program for students who want to swim with sharks, but don't want to run for government office.

Office hours: 1. (*pf.*) The only times when there is no risk that a student will interrupt your work with questions about the course or assignments.

2. (*st.*) The only times during which it is risky to walk by a professor's office.

3. (*adm.*) The hours posted on a professor's door which indicate the most likely times to find them in the coffee shop.

Open-book test: 1. (*pf.*) An exam that requires the student to apply information to unique scenarios rather than simply repeat the information. Often given by professors who enjoy the sound a book makes when it is opened for the first time.

2. (*st.*) The only reason to buy the required textbook.

3. (*adm.*) A means of selling textbooks written by the faculty. (see student definition)

Oral Presentation: 1. (*pf.*) The reason someone invented PowerPoint.

2. (*st.*) The reason someone invented YouTube.

Orientation: The period before the start of classes; when students get acquainted with the challenges of parking, visit the library for the first and last time, while being told a fairy-tale version of college life.

Out-of-state: 1. (*pf.*) Depending on where you live, they are the best type of conferences.

2. (*st.*) The destination for Spring Break.

3. (*adm.*) The reason to charge some students triple the tuition of others.

Paraphrase: 1. (*pf.*) The process of taking someone else's idea and expressing it in your own words, while giving the creator credit for their work.

2. (*st.*) A less than fully qualified phrase.

Parking permit: An expensive hunter's license for a place to park on campus.

Participation: 1. (*pf.*) The act of taking part in a class by coming prepared, asking questions, and contributing to the discussion; usually only performed by the instructor.

2. (*st.*) Sitting in class.

3. (*adm.*) Sitting in a meeting.

Party: 1. (*pf.*) A group of persons gathered for a specific purpose, such as a political party.

2. (*st.*) A social gathering for watching sports, flirting, and excessive consumption of alcoholic beverages.

3. (*adm.*) The person suing the university.

Pass/Fail: 1. (*pf.*) A grading system in which a student either passes or fails a course.

2. (*st.*) G.P.A. protection against courses that require actual work and learning.

Pets: The only members of your family you like, who make great excuses for non-attendance with certain professors. They also have a time-honored proclivity for destroying homework.

Ph.D.: 1. (*pf.*) A doctorate degree, specifically called a "doctor of philosophy" degree. Awarded to approximately one percent of the U.S. adult population.

2. (*st.*) Piled higher and deeper.

3. (*adm.*) Also called a terminal degree, but not because you are likely to die from the work, although it could happen . . . .

Philosophy: A degree where you say at your job, "Why do you want fries with that?"

Physical Education / PE: The subject that took the fun times of recess and turned it into course work.

Physics: The branch of science that uses unbelievably complicated formulas to illustrate playing with a ball.

Physiology: A major, similar to anatomy, taken by students who want to study sex and become physicians. (see MEDICINE)

Placement test: 1. (*pf.*) A test given to a student prior to enrolling in a course, to ensure all students in the course have similar knowledge or proficiency.

2. (*st.*) A test used to keep students attending college longer.

3. (*adm.*) A tool to increase the number of classes a student will need to pay to attend.

Plagiarize: (*pf.*) 1. Stealing the work of another person.

2. (*st.*) A shortcut for writing research papers.

3. (*adm.*) The new dirty word on campuses.

Platform: 1. (*pf.*) A software program that creates an environment for specific activities.

2. (*st.*) Really tall, high-heeled shoes.

3. (*adm.*) Where the guest speaker stands.

Point of View: 1. (*pf.*) The voice the author uses to discuss the topic in an essay or research paper.

The pronoun "I" is used to represent a first person point of view.

2. (*st.*) A particular attitude towards a matter.

From my point of view, multiple-choice tests are preferred over essays.

3. (*adm.*) The position from which something is observed.

From the chancellors' point of view, all he sees is the beach.

Points: 1. (*pf.*) The means by which professors assign grades based on the completeness of the assignment rather than effort involved.

2. (*st.*) A gesture to direct someone's attention, usually by using the index finger.

3. (*adm.*) Important items on the meeting's agenda.

Policy: 1. (*pf.*) A set of actions adopted ahead of time which determine responses to reoccurring events. For example, a late policy for student submissions after the due date, which specifies the penalties involved, usually short of flogging.

2. (*st.*) A rule to be challenged.

3. (*adm.*) The rules that must be kept by the faculty, and will be bent by tuition-paying students.

Political Science: The discipline concerned with systems of government, analysis of political activity, and international relationships. (a.k.a. the study of organized crime.)

Politically correct: Language that is inoffensive, nondiscriminatory, and unbiased according to people who are none of these things.

Pop Quiz: 1. (*pf.*) An attempt by professors to ensure that students stay current with the assigned reading in a course.

2. (*st.*) A major source of students' nightmares and the reason there will always be prayer in schools.

3. (*adm.*) The teaching activity that results in students hiding in the library.

Portfolio: 1. (*pf.*) The compilation of student work assembled for the purpose of evaluating the quality of the student's academic achievement. It is used to determine if the student has met graduation requirements.

2. (*st.*) The college version of a science fair project. Completed with the same lack of independence that helped the student graduate from high school.

3. (*adm.*) The stocks held by the retirement fund.

PowerPoint: 1. (*pf.*) A form of torture used in lectures and meetings.

2. (*st.*) A cheaper alternative to Photoshop.

3. (*adm.*) The means of impressing others with colorful charts and graphs while avoiding printing costs.

Practicum: A course that involves working in the area of study and using the knowledge and skills that have been learned in school while paying the college for the privilege to do so and collecting no salary from the place of employment. (see INTERNSHIP)

Pregnancy: 1. (*pf.*) A common consequence of engaging in certain extracurricular activities.

2. (*st.*) The best excuse for puking in class.

3. (*adm.*) The reason visiting professors must be hired.

Prelims: 1. (*pf.*) An abbreviation of "Preliminary Examinations" in which a doctoral student takes a comprehensive exam to qualify for *candidacy* and earns the distinction of ABD. (see ABD).

2. (*st.*) The reason it may be possible to die from a Ph.D. (see PH.D.)

3. (*adm.*) The thing that comes before lims.

Prerequisite: 1. (*pf.*) A course which must be taken before enrolling in a higher-level course, or a course that requires prior knowledge.

2. (*st.*) The thing that comes before a requisite.

3. (*adm.*) A means of collecting tuition for lower division classes taught by lower-paid graduate assistants.

Print: 1. (*pf.*) To write clearly without joining the letters as one does with cursive writing.

2. (*st.*) An outdated media for books, assignments, and journals.

3. (*adm.*) The required form for all meeting agendas, requests for reimbursement, and research proposals.

Probation: 1. (*pf.*) A condition placed on a student when their grades fall below a certain GPA.

2. (*st.*) A career for people who don't care if anyone likes them.

3. (*adm.*) Assistant professorships.

Procrastination: 1. (*pf.*) The ability to be busy doing activities a person can do at any time in order to avoid doing the thing they are supposed to be doing right now. i.e. Putting soup cans in alphabetical order rather than grading student essays.

2. (*st.*) The ability to withstand the urge to do anything productive.

3. (*adm.*) The ability to avoid decision-making when someone is waiting for an answer.

Professor: 1. (*pf.*) Opposite of confessor.

2. (*st.*) A person who talks in someone else's sleep.

3. (*adm.*) Employees with expensive student loans.

Professor Emeritus: 1. (*pf.*) A distinguished, retired professor who continues to teach occasionally, but is immune from most of the higher-ed bullshit.

2. (*st.*) A really old professor who still teaches one course every year or so.

3. (*adm.*) A professor who no longer needs to impress anyone.

Proofread: 1. (*pf.*) The action taken immediately after sending an email.

2. (*st.*) What professors do while grading papers.

3. (*adm.*) Reading the evidence.

Protest: 1. (*pf.*) A traditional activity frequently engaged in by students who believe it is part of their liberal education to demonstrate their support for social justice.

2. (*st.*) A professional test.

3. (*adm.*) A noble cause when engaged in by students. A potential source of embarrassment when engaged in by faculty.

Provost: 1. (*pf.*) A senior administrative officer at colleges and universities who oversees committees and makes decisions in exchange for a six-figure salary.

2. (*st.*) A professional vost.

3. (*adm.*) Quicker than a fast-moving metal projectile. More formidable than a rail transport. Able to vault multi-story buildings with a single effort.

Psychology: The degree program in which students learn to help other people with their shit, while they avoid fixing their own.

Public Administration: The branch of political science that teaches future high-level bureaucrats to take government policies for building a horse and end up with something that resembles a camel.

Publication: 1. (*pf.*) The value placed on a professor by tenure committees, promotion boards, and other professors.

2. (*st.*) Things in libraries.

3. (*adm.*) A standard on which a university is judged by other universities.

Qualitative: A type of research that explores how people feel about their life.

Quantitative: A type of research that tells people how to feel about their life.

Quarter: 1. (*pf.*) An alternative to semesters. A quarter is approximately 10 weeks long.

2. (*st.*) A coin worth twenty-five cents.

3. (*adm.*) One-fourth of something.

Question: 1. (*pf.*) The pursuit of knowledge through inquiry.

2. (*st.*) What professors put on exams to test students' knowledge.

3. (*adm.*) A means of delaying reimbursement on expense accounts.

Quiet: 1. (*pf.*) What libraries used to offer in addition to books.

2. (*st.*) Putting a cell phone in airplane mode.

3. (*adm.*) Evidence that the person who just walked into the room was the subject of the conversation in that room.

Quiz: 1. (*pf.*) A brief test of knowledge.

2. (*st.*) An exercise in using Google serendipitously on a smartphone.

3. (*adm.*) Asking questions at a meeting.

Quote: 1. (*pf.*) A passage written with such precision that paraphrasing the material would compromise its elegance. Easily identified by quotation marks and citations which provide attribution.

2. (*st.*) A shortcut for writing research papers.

3. (*adm.*) The bid or estimate for a particular job or services.

R

Reality: 1. (*pf.*) The leading cause of stress among college professors.

2. (*st.*) The difficult time after the alcohol has worn off and the student realizes their parents will not always pay their bills.

3. (*adm.*) Life without prescription medication.

Reason: 1. (*pf.*) To think, understand, and form judgments by a process of logic. The ability is what professors hope to instill in their students.

2. (*st.*) An explanation as to why a paper is turned in late.

Recreation Center: 1. (*pf.*) The best place to go for exercise when you can't have sex.

2. (*st.*) The best place to go for exercise when you can't have sex.

3. (*adm.*) A fitness club on campus that allows additional fees to be charged to student accounts.

Reference: 1. (*pf.*) A list of the sources provided at the end of a manuscript so other people can read the same boring bullshit used in writing said manuscript.

2. (*st.*) Alluding to a meme.

3. (*adm.*) People who will swear a job applicant is the best person for the job.

Refund: 1. (*pf.*) Getting an extension on a research grant.

2. (*st.*) Money to go shopping when you drop a course.

3. (*adm.*) Funding again.

Registrar: 1. (*pf.*) The official keeper of student records who demands that college professors take attendance like a kindergarten teacher.

2. (*st.*) The office where students can add classes they have heard were easy A's, and drop or

withdraw from classes due to illness, family emergencies, and stupidity.

Religious Studies: A degree program for people who believe they will become employed after graduation if it is the will of their deity.

Required readings: 1. (*pf.*) The books that student must buy and read for a specific course.

2. (*st.*) Optional shit to read if you are really, really bored.

3. (*adm.*) Books sold by the campus bookstore.

Research: 1. (*pf.*) The magical act whereby professors pull habits out of a rat.

2. (*st.*) Reading Wikipedia.

3. (*adm.*) The most important source of revenue for the college that also is the basis of awarding tenure to assistant professors.

Research question: 1. (*pf.*) A short, specific, and debatable question which is the focus of the study. Not to be confused with "What the hell are you doing?" (see QUALITATIVE RESEARCH)

2. (*st.*) A short, specific, and debatable question that asks, "What the hell are you doing?"

Review: 1. (*pf.*) The formal assessment by a peer of a research manuscript where the goal is to find reasons for not publishing the article.

2. (*st.*) The skimming of notes and textbook shortly before a test that takes the place of actual study.

3. (*adm.*) The formal assessment of an expense report in which there is always some reason it cannot be paid until next month.

Reviewer: 1. (*pf.*) A professor who attempts to impress others by finding fault in the scholarship of their peers.

2. (*st.*) A person who attempts to impress others by finding fault in popular movies.

3. (*adm.*) A person who attempts to impress others by finding fault in the course curriculum.

Rewrite: 1. (*pf.*) An opportunity to advance the learning of a student when they can supply a rationale that is more substantive than that they don't like their grade.

2. (*st.*) A student's right to correct mistakes pointed out by the professor after submitting a rough draft.

Rubric: 1. (*pf.*) A document that articulates the expectations for an assignment by listing the criteria, and describing the levels of quality from excellent to poor with assigned point values.

2. (*st.*) The guy who invented the colorful cubic puzzle.

Sample: 1. *(pf.)* To take a representative group out of a population in order to conduct research.

2. *(st.)* Tasting the food, beer, or wine rather than taking a serving.

Sarcasm: The ability to insult idiots without them realizing it.

Scholarly writing: 1. *(pf.)* Academic writing that is similar in precision to technical writing and is devoid of anthropomorphisms, biases, and clichés.

2. *(st.)* Academic writing that is similar in precision to technical writing and is devoid of creativity, interest, and humor.

3. *(adm.)* That which results in publications.

Scholarship: 1. (*pf.*) An academic study of interest only to the scholar conducting it.

2. (*st.*) A grant or payment to support a student's education that didn't come from the student's parents.

3. (*adm.*) Cruise ships for academics.

Science: An academic major for people who are good at math and think lab coats are sexy.

Seminar: 1. (*pf.*) A class focused on a specific topic and discussed by a small group of advanced students.

2. (*st.*) An elitist form of education for a group of teacher's pets, not available to everyone.

3. (*adm.*) A conference or meeting conducted to provide training.

Senior: 1. (*pf.*) Someone who is higher than the person who is junior.

2. (*st.*) A student who is in their last year of college and their first year of apathy.

3. (*adm.*) People who are wiser than younger people.

Skills: 1. *(pf.)* The ability to do something well; expertise in a specific area.

In college, students need to develop time management, technical writing, and critical thinking skills.

2. *(st.)* An ability acquired through deliberate, systematic, and sustained effort.

Because of the skills I have attained through practice, I have the highest score on Grand Theft Auto.

Slippers: 1. *(pf.)* Comfortable footwear appropriate when teaching an online course and grading papers at home. Never worn in public.

2. *(st.)* Comfortable footwear, which makes a statement about early morning or late night courses. Often worn in the classroom along with pajama pants.

Smart phone (Smartphone): 1. *(pf.)* A handheld mini-computer that can send and receive phone calls.

2. *(st.)* A cell phone that is smarter than my professor.

3. (*adm.*) A means of having 24/7 contact with faculty no matter where they are hiding.

Social sciences: A collection of disciplines in which people realize society is shit, and that's why they will never run out of shit to research.

Social Work: A feel-good discipline for professional co-dependents who believe they should teach poor people how to live.

Sociology: The study of human behavior, development, organizations, and institutions in the quest to know why people act stupid.

Sophomore: The class of students most annoyed by freshmen.

Spring Break: A vacation period in early spring where students learn new skills they will not brag about to their parents, but will post to their Facebook page. (see FACEBOOK)

Statistics: The best class to attend if a doctor gives you only days to live, because one hour in a stats class will feel like an eternity. (see ETERNITY)

Stress: 1. (*pf.*) The tension created while grading a student's submission where one wants to protect society from idiots, but also needs to avoid negative course evaluations in hopes of tenure.

2. (*st.*) The tension created when faced with the choice between going to a party and studying for a test.

3. (*adm.*) The confusion created when a parent's mind overrides their natural instinct to slap their offspring who aren't attending classes.

Student: 1. (*pf.*) The favorite experimental subject for professors trying to conduct research on a small budget.

2. (*st.*) The role played by most people for 13 years of their life, which some people turn into a position for more than 30 years.

3. (*adm.*) A source of revenue.

Student Government: A small group of student leaders who vote on aspects of student life as they learn that college administrators are puppet masters.

Student Loan: The only thing students fear more than death and likely to last longer than a graduate's professional career.

Study: The art of texting and eating while watching television with a textbook nearby.

Stupid question: 1. (*pf.*) Any question that can be answered with, "It's in the syllabus."

2. (*st.*) When a professor asks, "Did you read the syllabus?"

Submission: 1. (*pf.*) A homework assignment, essay, or research paper turned in for a grade.

2. (*st.*) Giving in to a professor's pleas to "please read the syllabus."

3. (*adm.*) Turning in an expense report.

Success: The opposite of failure and the result of hard work.

Suggested Readings: 1. (*pf.*) A book list diligently prepared by professors and created to improve a student's learning in a course.

2. (*st.*) A list of books no one buys.

3. (*adm.*) Wasted space on the shelves in the bookstore.

Summarize 1. (*pf.*) The ability to take a long passage, interpret the significance of the main points, analyze the arguments, and reduce it to the most important elements.

2. (*st.*) Related to hot weather from June to August.

Summer school: An optional semester.

Syllabus: 1. (*pf.*) A document painstakingly prepared by a professor detailing every aspect of a course. Archival only. Never read by students.

2. (*st.*) Italian for a funny looking bus.

3. (*adm.*) A legal document that serves to cover a professor's ass.

Synonym: A word used in place of the one you can't spell.

TBA 1. (*pf.*) To be announced.

2. (*st.*) The initials of the most overworked professor in the entire college. The instructor responsible for teaching nearly half of the classes offered.

Teacher: The person who helps you solve the problems you didn't have before you were put in the class.

Teaching Assistant (TA): A graduate student paid to do a professor's dirty work.

Technology: The ability to make mistakes that take engineers to solve.

Teenager: A person who is better prepared for a zombie apocalypse than tomorrow's English exam.

Tenure: 1. (*pf.*) The point at which a professor has almost as much power as an administrator at a university.

2. (*st.*) A male opera singer.

3. (*adm.*) Teflon for professors.

Test: 1. (*pf.*) Finding the limits.

Your emails are a test of my patience.

2. (*st.*) A form of torture devised by professors to ruin a student's social life.

I can't party because I have a test tomorrow.

Textbook: 1. (*pf.*) A boring book written by boring professors to teach boring classes to bored students.

2. (*st.*) An outrageously expensive boring book.

Thanksgiving: 1. (*pf.*) The fall holiday that results in students celebrating 5 days of the 4-day weekend.

2. (*st.*) The reason no laundry is done on campus in November.

3. (*adm.*) The beginning of the "holiday season" which launches the latest fund raising campaign.

Theater: A useful degree for people who want to act as if they are employable.

Thesis: True Happiness Ended Since It Started.

Thinking: 1. (*pf.*) A behavior expected of students.

2. (*st.*) What professors say they want, but what they mean is mind reading.

3. (*adm.*) What administrators are doing when they don't appear to be doing anything.

"Thinking is the hardest work there is, which is probably the reason why so few engage in it." ~Henry Ford.

Time Management: 1. (*pf.*) The ability to use one's time effectively, especially in regards to studying and writing assignments.

2. (*st.*) The ability to use one's time effectively so as not to miss the latest movie.

3. (*adm.*) The rarest ability on campus.

Time Out: 1. (*pf.*) Exceeding the allotted amount of time for completing a graduate degree.

2. (*st.*) A break during a sports game.

3. (*adm.*) Sick leave.

Tomorrow: 1. (*pf.*) The mantra of procrastinators. "A mystical place where 99% of all human productivity, motivation and achievements are stored." ~Author Unknown

2. (*st.*) The best time to do everything that was due today.

Transcript: 1. (*pf.*) A written copy of something that was once said.

2. (*st.*) A copy of the list of courses and grades required for certain activities such as licensure.

3. (*adm.*) An official report of a student's courses, grades received, and dates of attendance, which provides a small but life-long source of revenue.

Transfer: 1. (*pf.*) Accepting credits from another college or university.

2. (*st.*) A means of using more than one bus, but only paying once.

3. (*adm.*) Allowing a student to receive credit for a course they paid for elsewhere.

Tuition: 1. (*pf.*) What students mistakenly believe pays the salaries of professors. (see GRANT)

2. (*st.*) The world's most expensive bar tab.

3. (*adm.*) The cost of job training.

Tutor: 1. (*pf.*) A private instructor who teaches a single subject to an individual student or small group.

3. (*st.*) The person responsible for the student passing the course.

3. (*adm.*) Looking up "how to" videos on YouTube.

U

Umbrella: *(pf.)* A portable, circular covering used to protect against inclement weather.

2. *(st.)* The only use for student newspapers.

Undergraduate: A high school graduate attending college in order to avoid getting a real job for another 4 years.

Underground: 1. *(pf.)* That which is below ground, such as a basement.

2. *(st.)* Coffee beans that need more grinding.

3. *(adm.)* That which is hidden or secret, such as conspiracies.

Unique: 1. (*pf.*) One of a kind. An *absolute* word similar to "complete" and "perfect," and should never be used with the word "very."
The artifact was unique.
2. (*st.*) Not typical or common.
She has very unique flirting skills.

University: 1. (*pf.*) A group of schools that offer undergraduate as well as graduate degrees.
2. (*st.*) The school after high school.
3. (*adm.*) An institution of higher learning that naturally comes at a higher price.

University Studies: A college major for undecided college majors.

Upload: 1. (*pf.*) The simple and rapid transfer of data from one computer to another.
2. (*st.*) The lengthy and complicated process of turning in an assignment to an online course which usually involves multiple calls to the help desk.
3. (*adm.*) The opposite of download.

Upper Division: The opposite of lower division.

Vacation: 1. (*pf.*) The reason professional conferences are held in Hawaii.

2. (*st.*) The reason for Spring Break and Thanksgiving weekends.

3. (*adm.*) The reason it is easier to park on campus during the summer.

Valedictorian 1. (*pf.*) The student who graduated at the top of their high school class and believes the professor will be impressed.

2. (*st.*) The student who acts the wildest during their freshman year in college.

3. (*adm.*) Scholarship recipients.

Vehicle: 1. (*pf.*) A means of transmission or passage.

The lecture is the traditional vehicle of imparting knowledge.

2. (*st.*) A means by which something is carried.

My bicycle is my primary vehicle to campus.

3. (*adm.*) The means by which something is conveyed.

Differences in salaries is a vehicle for identifying the worth of the person to the university.

Vent 1. (*pf.*) To let off steam or pressure.

Sometimes when I am grading papers, I vent on Twitter.

2. (*st.*) The opening in the wall that allows for air in the room to be exchanged with air from the heater or air conditioning in another part of the building.

3. (*adm.*) A slit in the back or side of a garment.

Vice: 1. (*pf.*) A type of deputy or second in command who takes the place of the primary in their absence.

The vice-provost will attend the meeting instead.

2. (*st.*) An immoral habit that is practiced as often as possible during college.

3.(*adm.*) Something that took place in Miami.

Visa: 1. (*pf.*) An endorsement on a passport that allows the student to enter, leave, or stay in the US if they enroll at a qualified educational institution.

2. (*st.*) A credit card.

Visiting professor: A temporary gig for professors who failed to earn tenure at their previous college or university.

Wage: 1. (*pf.*) A fixed regular payment, computed on an hourly basis for graduate assistants.

2. (*st.*) Enough money to keep working, not enough money to call it a living.

Wait Staff (Waiter or Waitress): An off-campus position for college students majoring in the humanities.

Wake: 1. (*pf.*) The preferable condition of students in the classroom.

2. (*st.*) A good excuse not to attend class, even if you barely knew the deceased.

3. (*adm.*) The trail of disturbed water left by a cruise ship.

Walk: 1. (*pf.*) Shorthand expression for graduating. *The student walked across the stage to receive his degree.*

2. (*st.*) The exercise one gets from parking on campus.

3. (*adm.*) Allowing a job candidate to go to another school when they demand more money.

Wand: 1. (*pf.*) The long, thin stick used to point to portions of the chalkboard or overhead projector in ancient times.

2. (*st.*) The long, thin stick with magical properties used by students at Hogwarts.

Want: A desire, often confused with a necessity.

War: 1. (*pf.*) The only time Americans learn anything about geography.

2. (*st.*) The first deck-builder card game.

3. (*adm.*) A time to offer distance learning to our troops, paid for by the Department of Defense.

Warn: Informing a student that their attempts to lie, cheat, and ignore the rules may indicate they should run for Congress rather than continue in the course.

Warp: 1. (*pf.*) The twisting or distortion of the syllabus to fit a student's needs.

2. (*st.*) A factor of the speed of light at which the USS Enterprise can travel.

3. (*adm.*) When something (or someone) becomes bent out of shape.

Wealth: 1. (*pf.*) That which was abandoned in search of scholarship.

2. (*st.*) The primary source of "first world problems."

3. (*adm.*) That which must be tapped for new buildings, endowed chairs, and scholarships.

Weather: 1. (*pf.*) An event of nature that provided more days off in high school than it does in college.

2. (*st.*) Something subject to change without notice.

3. (adm.) To survive a storm.

The assistant professor weathered the vote for tenure.

Web: 1. (*pf.*) The complex system of interconnected elements that often involves a trap or dangerous situation. (a.k.a. campus politics)

2. (*st.*) The Internet.

3. (*adm.*) An artifact made by spiders which is the reason exterminators are kept on retainer.

Wedding: The act or ceremony of marrying. Routinely scheduled during a difficult course and busy work load.

Weed: 1. (*pf.*) Cannabis.

2. (*st.*) Marijuana.

3. (*adm.*) To remove something that detracts from the whole.

"We need to weed out the deadwood among the faculty.

Weekend: 1. (*pf.*) The mythical period of time in which all work can be accomplished, including grading, research, and writing.

2. (*st.*) The period of time in which there is a seventy percent chance of alcohol consumption with corresponding periods of making poor decisions.

3. (*adm.*) A time to relax and send emails to faculty with insane demands which creates the appearance of doing actual work.

Weird: 1. (*pf.*) Either a derogatory remark or a compliment. Technically, it refers to something out of the ordinary. Also known as people in Portland, OR and Austin, TX.

2. (*st.*) Any professor who expects students not to cut-and-paste from the Internet.

3. (*adm.*) An alternative to that which is illegal, immoral, or fattening.

Whine: 1. (*pf.*) The quality of a student's speech which occurs when the student isn't told he or she is wonderful.

2. (*st.*) The quality of a professor's speech which occurs when the professor complains about their research studies.

3. (*adm.*) The quality of a Board of Director's speech which occurs when a professor writes a book about the politics in higher education.

Whiskey: 1. (*pf.*) The only time it doesn't matter whether the glass is half-empty or half-full.

2. (*st.*) The best way to avoid water-borne contaminants.

3. (*adm.*) An unacceptable expense report expenditure.

Who: 1. (*pf.*) The World Health Organization.

2. (*st.*) The Time Lord from Gallifrey.

3. (*adm.*) Referring to a person or persons.

The student attends class, but the parents are who pay the tuition.

Wicked: Evil or morally bad except in Boston, MA where it is a substitution for the word "very". In Boston, something that is "wicked awesome" means it is fabulous.

Wikipedia: 1. (*pf.*) A major source of the plagiarism found in student papers.

2. (*st.*) Kind of like an encyclopedia, but better because everyone contributes to it.

3. (*adm.*) The one website that can be found on the Internet history of everyone on campus.

Windows: 1. (*pf.*) The period of time when something is available.

There is only a three day window to send in my grant proposal.

2. (*st.*) A computer operating system.

3. (*adm.*) An architectural feature of the best offices on campus.

Wine: 1. (*pf.*) A beverage made from fermented grape juice. Sometimes made from other fruit juices as well, such as berries.

2. (*st.*) To entertain someone by offering them food and drinks. *The football coach wined and dined the best football player applicants.*

3. (*adm.*) A benefit of offering programs in Viticulture and Enology.

Winter: 1. (*pf.*) The coldest season of the year in the northern hemisphere when students attend classes dressed for artic excursions.

2. (*st.*) The college quarter with the most holidays.

3. (*adm.*) The coldest season of the year in the northern hemisphere when faculty leave their

heated homes, to drive in heated cars, to their heated offices on campus, and complain as though they walked here.

Wise: 1. (*pf.*) Professors.

2. (*st.*) Delusional professors.

3. (*adm.*) Retired professors.

Wit: The ability to make people laugh without resorting to profanity, insult, or potty humor.

Withdrawal: 1. (*pf.*) The transcript notation for when a student bails from a course he or she is otherwise failing.

2. (*st.*) A flawed birth control method.

4. (*adm.*) The transcript notation for when a student received neither a grade nor a refund.

Wizard: 1. (*pf.*) A help feature of a software program that automates tasks because programmers know most people are idiots.

2. (*st.*) The student in the course who knows all the answers as if by magic.

3. (*adm.*) Someone with supernatural abilities.

Women's Studies: A degree program for people who want to be professional feminists.

Wordy: 1. (*pf.*) Student writing that is characterized by, seen as, and identified with, using far too many words when only a few words are necessary, desired, or required. Often leads to repeating words in a redundant manner or fashion.

2. (*st.*) It is like being a foodie, but with words.

3. (*adm.*) Speeches.

Work: 1. (*pf.*) The activity that pays for your anti-depressants, psychotherapy, and child support.

2. (*st.*) The activity that pays for your video games, cell phones, and vacations.

3. (*adm.*) The activity avoid at all costs by faculty and students.

Work-Study: The program for undergraduate students where students pretend to work and the university pretends they have jobs.

Writer: 1. (*pf.*) The person who enjoys playing god with their own little world.

2. (*st.*) A person who keeps a journal or blogs.

3. (*adm.*) The person who requests grant money.

Writing Lab/Writing Center: 1. (*pf.*) The resource for students who need a little extra help with writing at the college level.

2. (*st.*) Unpaid proofreaders.

3. (*adm.*) Where students are sent by professors who don't understand fifth grade writing.

Wrong: 1. (*pf.*) Not the correct answer.

2. (*st.*) Professors who do not give partial credit for trying.

3. (*adm.*) Professors who think they should keep all their grant money for their research.

Xavier: Head master of the school for mutants on The X-Men.

Xenophobia: An unreasonable fear or hatred of foreigners or strangers.

Xerox: 1. (*pf.*) Trademarked copying machine. Also used to identify something that was "copied." *Here is a Xerox of the syllabus.*

2. (*st.*) An evil multinational company where old people made a killing on the stock market.

Xylophone: 1. (*pf.*) A musical instrument.

2. (*st.*) The only word most students can recall as a word starting with the letter "x."

Yahoo: 1. (*pf.*) The name in Swift's "Gulliver's Travels" for an uncultivated or boorish person.

2. (*st.*) An Internet search engine used by the same.

3. (*adm.*) A cheer.

Yawn: 1. (*pf.*) To open the mouth somewhat involuntarily with a prolonged deep inhalation, often seen during commencement speeches.

2. (*st.*) A side effect of attending class.

3. (*adm.*) A side effect of attending open house.

Year: A period of 365 or 366 days in the Gregorian calendar, which can seem much longer when taking difficult classes.

Yes/No Question: A dichotomous question with only two possible choices for response regardless of the rationale behind the selection.

Yesterday: 1. (*pf.*) The deadline for all student complaints.

2. (*st.*) The deadline for the assignment being written this weekend.

3. (*adm.*) A song by The Beatles.

Yoga 1. (*pf.*) A form of exercise that relieves stress and resembles the positions taken by faculty members when they clip their toenails.

2. (*st.*) A style of sexy pants.

3. (*adm.*) The little green Jedi master in Star Wars.

Youth: The age group who know the answers to life, the universe, and everything.

Zany: Absurdly or whimsically comical.

This is a zany dictionary.

Zealot: The worst example from which to judge a religion or culture.

Zen: A practice which emphasizes enlightenment by means of meditation and direct intuitive insights. Only truly practiced by cats.

Zero: Naught, nothing, nada. The lowest possible grade on an exam or paper. Rare, but not impossible to earn.

ZigZag: 1. (*pf.*) A brand of cigarette paper for people who roll their own cigarettes.

2. (*st.*) A brand of thin paper used for rolling joints.

3. (*adm.*) A line characterized by repeated sharp turns to one side and then the other–often seen when running spell check.

Zodiac: 1. (*pf.*) The division of the sky into twelve parts with each part named for a nearby constellation.

2. (*st.*) A sign that can predict love, fortune, and adversity, but not grades, jobs, or parking tickets.

Zombie: 1. (*pf.*) A tall mixed drink consisting of white rum, golden rum, dark rum, 151-proof rum, lime juice, pineapple juice, apricot brandy, and sugar.

2. (*st.*) The walking dead. Often resembling college students.

3. (*adm.*) A dead person who is animated but in a trance who moves around as if unconscious. Often confused with professors who refuse to retire.

Zonked: 1. (*pf.*) The result of grading papers late at night.

2. (*st.*) The result of studying for class late at night.

3. (*adm.*) The result of working on budgets late at night.

Zool: 1. (*pf.*) Also known as Zoological.

2. (*st.*) Short for zoologist. Not to be confused with Zuul, the demigod worshipped as a servant to Gozer the Gozerian, who haunted the apartment of Dana Barrett on Ghostbusters.

Zoology: A degree program for people who are ape-shit about animals.

Zzzz: Used to represent a student sleeping during a lecture and indicate the sound of snoring.

Acknowledgements

I surround myself with people who encourage my writing, my humor, and giving in to my inner snark. First on that list is my good friend and editor, Susan Frager. In addition to her editorial wisdom, she lets me know when something is only funny to me.

I have also found that getting together with other authors, published and unpublished, is the best investment of my time outside of actual writing. As my writing skills grow, these people continue to push me to excel in everything I put on paper.

The primary place where I get a balance of encouragement along with the picking apart of my work, is the *SW WA/OR Write to Publish* critique group, founded by Linda Stirling, author of several books including "Signature Energy, The Vibration of You."

I want to thank and give hat tips to my fellow authors in this critique group:

Karla von Huben, author of several books, most recently "The Youngest Elf and Other Stories: Further Adventures."

Lelia Rose Foreman, author of "Tales of Talifer."

Kumiko Olson, author of "From Tokyo To America: Seven Times Down Eight Times Up."

Jon Drury, author of "Lord, I Feel So Small."

I have also received great advice from Andi Crockford, James Chesky, Jesse McClure, Amanda Cherry, Erika Work and Adam Stewart and wish them well on their writing journeys.

I want to thank the *Coffee House Writers Group*, Portland OR with co-founders Elizabyth (Burtis) Harrington, and Mark Harrington. Elizabyth is the author of "Demonology: Book of Gabriel."

Vargus Pike, poet extraordinaire and his most recent collection: "July Song." Heather Self, author of "Backbeat." Catherine Adee, who is writing several books, which I am eagerly awaiting. And the rest of the writers, who laughed where they should and provided good advice when it wasn't funny.

About the Author

Ilana Lehmann is like no one you have met before. A high school drop-out who went on to earn a Ph.D., she was born and raised in San Diego, CA and has lived at over 50 addresses across the United States.

She has a bachelor's degree in psychology and a master's degree in guidance and counseling with an emphasis on community mental health. She earned her doctorate in Rehabilitation Counseling from Southern Illinois University.

Currently, she teaches research methods online to masters and doctoral students.

She is writing more books and promises to continue to write until she is no longer educational or entertaining. Dr. Lehmann is bossed around by her cat, Hobbes, and her corgi named Susie Derkins.

Help Wanted!

Did I leave out a definition?
Did I leave out a word that belongs in the dictionary?
Do you have an idea for another role?

If so, sent it to me and if I include it in the next edition, I will put your name in the acknowledgements section with a thank you for your input.

dictionary@mindmeldmedia.com

www.ingramcontent.com/pod-product-compliance
Lightning Source LLC
Chambersburg PA
CBHW051948290426
44110CB00015B/2155